To

Margaret

Dedicated to Sue Smith
of London

Sincere best wishes
from George

July 27th 2012

Contents

BEYOND THE GRAVE

Foreword

During late 2011, after much pressure from a certain Lincolnshire lady, I published 'Silent Footsteps'. It concerned all my paranormal experiences I'd had on haunted Lincolnshire World War II Airfields. I'm pleased to say the little book, pocket-sized, was well received by the public and I sold many copies, as well as giving some away to family and friends.

On the other side of the coin, I also had plenty of 'civvie' encounters. Four of them happened in Haworth, Brontë country, where I am a regular visitor. Just as in my airfield ones, I have had nine encounters with the unexplained but later, I remembered the Buckley Green one! (10). All these stories, though, began when I was in my late thirties/early forties, and up to the present day, April 2012. I am now 67 years old.

Woodfarm Cottage, where I live with my wife Helen, since 1976, is heavily haunted by a ghost we call 'Bill', but we have no idea if it's male or female! Usually, it's a mischievous spirit, but it does not like my daughter Samantha, who left home some time ago. Whenever she

3

entered our bedroom, she experienced awful feelings, which she cannot explain. My son Gary, when he was at home, was never affected.

'Bill' switches electrical gadgets on and off, hides things, only to reappear weeks later, and loves to make a noise in the cutlery tray!! I was in my son's old room once – now my 'office', when I heard a commotion downstairs in the kitchen – the sounds of knives and forks being noisily rustled about on the sink unit. I went down thinking Helen had returned, but the noise stopped abruptly and all the cutlery was neatly stacked in the tray. One thing 'Bill' did take a dislike to was 'Gordon the Gopher', a hand puppet my daughter owned and was always squeaking it! Gordon disappeared one day and we have never found it since, though I suspect Helen had something to do with it as she hates noisy objects!

So then, here are my encounters, plus two from other folk. I can offer no plausible explanation for what I saw – it just happened when I was least expecting it. I will begin with the Griffe Mill Ghost at Haworth because, after 14 years, this encounter still bugs me, and I'm determined to get to the bottom of it. My good friend, Sue Smith, of East Dulwich, London has been an invaluable help to me along the way, and I can't thank her enough.

Chapter One: Griffe Mill- Haworth area

Griffe Mill is a former textile mill which is now in ruins at the bottom of the valley below the village of Stanbury, and within about a quarter-mile from Ponden Mill. I first visited the ruins many years ago in the 1980s, when I first joined the Brontë Society. Nowadays, there is one three-storey wall remaining, various outbuildings and extensive fallen ruins inside. The small mill chimney still stands. There is a small goit (stream) that used to feed the waterwheel, but mostly it is covered in fallen masonry and old roof beams. It is indeed a dark and sinister place with the invasive elder trees growing up the through the ruins and stinging nettles everywhere. My first visit here was on a Brontë Society walk, and I visited several times since, in the company of others.   But it wasn't until the 21st December 1997, that this old mill would have such a profound effect on me, and one day before I was due to go home.

Most years, I come for a long weekend stay in Haworth just before Christmas, because of the atmosphere and the shop girls dressing up in authentic Victorian costume. And so it was, on the afternoon of the 20th December, found me having a quiet drink in the 'Black Bull' pub. It didn't stay quiet for long!

There was a young chap and his girlfriend stood at the bar, and an old chap, obviously local and tipsy with drink, making a fool of himself. Eventually the couple had had enough and went to sit down at the other end of the busy pub, but not before the old chap shouted: "I'm telling thee, t'mill at Griffe is haunted!!"

My ears pricked up at that! Where ghosts are concerned, I'm in. But I made the bad mistake of not following it up and approaching the drunk for more information. I could kick myself now because I could have saved myself a lot of hassle.

Next morning, after breakfast, I left my B & B and headed out towards Stanbury, 99% sure I was on a wasted journey. The weather was bitingly cold, gloomy and misty, but dead calm. It took me about three-quarters of an hour to reach Griffe Mill because the downhill route was very wet and spongy. It was even worse as I crossed over a wooden bridge and followed the stream bed, crossing over barbed wire obstacles and marshy bits. The main path hugs the hillside but I decided to be clever and follow the edge of the stream. My walking boots were soon caked up with clinging mud.

After what seemed like an age, I climbed over the extensive ruins of the old mill, on the alert for anything untoward. However, the only sound that came to my straining ears was the trickle from the goit. Eventually, I stood still and looked up at the 3-storey single wall that used to be the main entrance, and noted several old fireplaces dotted here and there, obviously the owners living quarters of long ago.

Standing there in the cold and stillness, I suddenly got the feeling I was being watched, and experienced a cold chill on my neck and down my spine. I whipped round, but saw only weeds, brambles and heaps of rubble. I turned back – and there she was!! Not three yards or slightly more away, was a little girl of about 8 or 9, dressed in 'funny' clothes. On her head she wore like an old fashioned scullery maid's lace cap, long, off-white apron over a dull grey dress almost down to her feet, on which were what looked like clogs. She was quite thin and average height, but what really arrested my gaze were her ice blue eyes and very long, curly ginger hair that fell down her back in masses of curls. "Who the hell are you?!" I just managed, getting over my shock.

The girl did not answer and we stood staring at each other for maybe 5-10 seconds. Suddenly, she smiled broadly, revealing brilliant white teeth – and then she was gone – vanished into thin air! No puff of smoke, no fading away – just gone!!

For ages, I just stood rooted to the spot, my whole body shaking. Eventually though, normality returned and I shakily left the mill and took the path out of the valley, having a much-needed coffee at nearby Ponden Mill.

Since that time, I have spent 14 years researching the little girl, finding out her name, even finding a family grave in Stanbury cemetery. It was three old pensioners who threw light on the haunting, but strangely enough, all three lived in separate communities, Stanbury, Haworth and Upper Marsh, but their stories tallied.

The story goes that a little girl from Oldfield, on the opposite side of the valley to Stanbury, and called Susannah Arabella Shackleton, did, on one dark December night, 21st December 1897, run down the steep hill from her home, to meet her dad coming off shift at Griffe Mill, fell into a large water tank and drowned. However, my research over the years, and using old drawings of the mill, shows no such location of a water tank, only a large gasometer. And there is no trace of a Susannah living in Oldfield at that time, which is a small hamlet. Furthermore, church records show there was no Susannah Arabella Shackleton living in Stanbury. The three old chaps said she was 9-12 when she died. The Susannah I found in the Stanbury area, lived at nearby Sladen Bridge, and she was last mentioned in the census as 21. Her parents and brother, killed in the First World War, all lie together in one grave in the hilltop Stanbury cemetery.

Over the ensuing years I have faced much hostility from locals, my being an 'outsider' and delving in Shackleton business. Back in 1998, an old woman, looking very much (and sounding!) like Norah Batty of 'Last of the Summer Wine' fame, threatened to assault me if I didn't clear off back to Lincolnshire! So what have they got to be afraid of? Was little Susannah really murdered by some well-known local man, and the crime was hushed up? Maybe the family was given a monetary bribe to keep quiet? Someday, with the help of Sue from London, I'll crack this case. I won't give up!!

Chapter Two: The Angry Lady - Haworth

This encounter was really weird to say the least, and it happened on the darkened streets of Haworth in the late 1990s, days before Christmas. I was stood in a throng of bystanders watching a church parade coming up Main Street, singing Christmas carols – and called a 'Torchlight Procession' – which is held most years, weather permitting.

There were hundreds of folks lining the streets waiting for the procession to arrive. I was stood near the 'Apothecary' shop, top of Main Street, and opposite the 'Black Bull' pub. At some point I glanced behind me and saw this young woman in her twenties, wearing Victorian clothes. She was bare-headed and wore a dark green dress with white frilled sleeves and neckline. I knew it was emerald green because I saw her in the same outfit the next day!

I guessed the girl must have worked in one of the shops, or even the Apothecary itself, as all the shop girls get dressed up in period costume for the festive season. It lends an air of realism to a Haworth Victorian Christmas. However, when I smiled at her, she looked really nasty towards me! I quickly turned round.

The following morning, after breakfast at my B & B, I decided on a short walk to Penistone Hill, and going by the Sunday School and Parsonage. As is normal for weekday Haworth, the streets were deserted apart from one or two early risers and delivery vehicles.

On Church Lane, I had just passed the main entrance into the cemetery, when I suddenly caught sight of a pound coin lying on the stone setts. "I'm having that!" I smiled to myself, and bent over to retrieve my bounty. Suddenly though, I noticed out of the corner of my eye, a person hurrying down the lane from the direction of the Parsonage. It was her – the sullen-looking young woman of the previous evening – and in the same dress! "Dammit!" I oathed under my breath. I straightened up, leaving the coin where it was, and began to walk slowly forwards. The girl scowled as she passed me, even though I said a cheery "Good Morning".

I looked round a few moments later, and to my dismay I saw her bending over the coin! I swore under my breath again, as I walked on a few yards, stopped, looked back, and the lane was empty! Where on earth could she have gone in those few moments?

I turned and walked back down towards St Michael's Church, assuming she was crossing the cemetery. To my amazement, and delight, the pound coin was still there! I scooped it up quickly then hurried to the cemetery gate. No sign of her - or inside the church. I hurried back to the church steps but Main Street was empty! I was flabbergasted; no way could she have covered so much distance in so short a time. I have no choice but to let this one remain 'on file' as not explained.

Chapter Three: Ponden Mill – Haworth area

For years, Ponden Mill was used as three floors of shops selling all sorts of household goods and gifts. It also had an excellent café/restaurant. Many are the times I have sat there with a coffee and eating large slabs of delicious sandwich cakes or Black Forest Gateau! I've also visited many times with Brontë Society friends. Sadly, the former woollen mill is now closed, the firm ceased trading.

Ponden Mill lies in a narrow valley below Stanbury and 'The Old Silent Inn' – the same wooded valley as Griffe Mill. I noticed the car park was about three-quarters full, but right near the mill, nearby is the man-made reservoir of Ponden Water, and Scar Top hamlet close by. There is a large, extensive car park one end of the mill, and on the other side of the road, a fast flowing tiny River Worth.

This particular hot day one AGM weekend in June 1999, I believe, I'd been for an exhausting trek up to nearby Ponden Kirk, on the moors. I decided to call into the café at Ponden Mill before beginning the uphill journey back to Stanbury, and eventually Haworth. I noticed the car park was about three-quarters full, but right near the mill, I saw a strange sight.

On a small expanse of bare parking area, I noticed a woman, oddly dressed in strange clothes, rather like the Victorian scullery maids in posh houses, scrubbing away at what I took to be a large blanket. Beside her was an old fashioned wicker basket full of clothes or whatever. What really intrigued me though, she was bending over this huge stone trough, similar to what cattle drink out of. I've come across many examples when I've been drystone walling and know they must weigh a ton. One of my gardening customers has one and the thickness of the stone is at 2-3 inches. "Haven't you heard of a washing machine, duck?" I called across to the woman as I walked past her to the mill entrance. She did not look round at my voice and totally ignored me.

When I got in the café and ordered refreshments, one of the waitresses brought it over to my table, and I laughingly mentioned my run-in with mystery woman. "Bit behind the times aren't you, making women hand wash garments in a stone trough?"

The girl looked nonplussed at me and said she knew of no-one employed at the mill who did that kind of work. I chuckled and had my refreshments. I would investigate!

However, once out of the mill and into the car park, I was shocked to see no woman or heavy trough. In their place was parked a Range Rover! I was gob-smacked! That woman, or any man for that matter, would not be able to move that monstrous trough by themselves – it would have at least required a large fork-lift truck.

I searched all around the car park that day, and behind the mill building, but found not a trace. Eventually I had to give up because a man and woman sat in a car were eyeing me suspiciously!

But who was the washer-woman? Was she a former employee at the mill in years gone by? But why wash garments outside in the open, anyway?

Chapter Four: Penistone Hill Cemetery - Haworth

This was very baffling. I'd visited Haworth new cemetery on many occasions, just to see the grave of London aeronaut Miss Lily Cove, who is said to haunt room number 7 at the 'Old White Lion' pub in Haworth.

Lily tragically died whilst jumping from a hot air balloon in the 1920s, whilst attending a gala day in Haworth. Her parachute failed to open in time as she was too low and she was killed in a field near Stanbury. You can't miss Lily's grave, it is large and a dull blue, as you enter the cemetery from the Haworth end (turnstile gate).   This particular day it was very cold and rough with frequent light rain, even though it was supposed to be summer! I was well wrapped up against the cold. But imagine my surprise as I left the cemetery and saw a woman dressed in a Roaring Twenties 'pudding basin' hat and thin 'rah-rah' skirt stood by Lily's grave, clutching a bunch of flowers. "The silly girl, she'll freeze to death!" I uttered as I stood and watched as the girl bent over and laid the flowers on Lily's grave. I had to turn away and start walking because the young woman began to walk towards me. I didn't want her getting agitated, thinking I was some pervert. I reached the turnstile gate just ahead of her.

I smilingly stood aside as she began to go through. I looked back at the cemetery for a brief moment and then quietly followed behind her. Only thing was, she was no longer there! I looked up and down the road, and also the rough path that leads up the hillside to the old quarries. Nothing! Where on earth could she have gone? In the time I'd glanced back at the cemetery to her freeing herself of the turnstile, was mere seconds.

I was determined to get an explanation. I'd go back and pick up the bouquet of flowers and see who they had been donated by. But when I breathlessly returned to Lily's gravestone, there were no flowers! In that moment the heavens opened and I had no choice but to dive under the thick rhododendron bushes for cover. I never did find that girl again. Was she a relative of Lily? Dressed in 1920s clothes, was it Lily herself? I'll never know.

LINCOLNSHIRE GHOSTS

Chapter Five: The Horseman –Wood-Enderby

Not far from the famous town of Woodhall Spa, and once the nearby home of 617 Squadron, Guy Gibson's Dambusters, lays two little villages either side of a small river. Haltham and Wood-Enderby, just off the edge of the fenlands of Lincolnshire.

One Bank Holiday Monday, on my motorcycle, I was taking a short cut from Woodhall to get to the aviation museum at East Kirkby, home to the Lancaster 'Just Jane', which taxis down the runway for visitors, but cannot take off as it's not classed as airworthy. This place is usually packed with visitors on a Bank Holiday, and the museum put on flying displays using other aircraft. I love visiting here.

On this particular warm day, I'd actually parked on the little bridge over the river, and was stood looking into the water for fish. The road is only minor and not much traffic used it.

I was thus engrossed when I looked up to see a man leading a horse and cart. He was walking, holding the reins of what looked to be a Shire horse, and the four wheeled cart was really old fashioned and used for hay carrying.

I realised the road wasn't wide enough for him to get by my

motorcycle, so I quickly wheeled it off the bridge and parked it on some rough ground nearby. I watched intently as the man, very old and barely able to walk, passed over the bridge and off he went down the road. I said "hello mate" as he walked by, but he never answered. If he did, I never heard him, as I was still wearing my crash helmet! Funnily enough, I also never heard a sound from either the horse clopping or the hard metal rims on the cart wheels. The old chap was wearing brown stripy sort of trousers, tied up near the bottom by string, big hob-nailed boots, waistcoat, striped white shirt, flat cap and a sort of neckerchief around his throat. What bit of hair he had was curly grey.

I watched him awhile until he went round a bend in the road, but when I mounted up and drove after him, both he, horse and cart had vanished into thin air! I nearly fell off my bike in shock! I have no explanation for this puzzle. My next encounter was even more bizarre!

Chapter Six: Unwanted Company

Way back in 1989, when I became self-employed as a gardener and drystone waller, I was tidying up quite a large and overgrown garden near the village of Welton, just north of Lincoln. I cannot mention the exact location in case it upsets the living relatives of the very old lady – now passed away – I worked for.

Another gardener had passed the work on to me, saying he was too busy to help her. As soon as I saw the state the place was in, I thought, "Yeah, right, you don't want hard work, old mate!" The place was a shambles, but I couldn't blame the old lady, at least she had tried to get someone over the years. Most people who came to look, she never saw again, except one. He spent about 2 hours there, then gave it up as a bad job!

I was a bit more ambitious. Having just started out in the trade, I needed to make a good impression and gain more customers by word of mouth, as well as advertising in local shops. So I set to with gusto but soon realised the enormity of what I had taken on. There were endless, deep rooted thistles and the invasive ground elder, some of which infested the bases of rose bushes. I got prickled galore!

Initially, I spent 4 hours the first day but in the weeks that followed, I only gave her 2 hours at a time, to fit around my other gardening jobs elsewhere. Finally, after nearly 2 months of hard graft, I'd got the garden looking spick and span, the old lady was very grateful indeed, as were the local residents walking by who often stopped to comment on my work. However, during autumn of that year, I gained a somewhat grumpy, pest of an old man who walked into the back garden one day and began to advise what I should be doing next! I suspected he was a friend of the old lady, so I tolerated him. It wasn't long though before he came into the garden on every one of my visits, puffing on an old pipe and repeatedly lighting it. He wore old gardening clothes, boots and flat cap. He looked to be very elderly and walked unsteady, using a home-made old walking stick.

"She's gone and let the vegetable patch go to pot," he once observed. "Tell her she needs to buy a load of well-rotted hoss muck for you to dig in." Another time he said I ought to be thinking about pruning the roses before it was too late in the season.

"I normally cut 'em off just above the second bud," he said.

"Do you now," I answered coldly. "Don't worry, I know what I'm doing."

He seemed to take offence at that and sullenly stomped off, muttering under his breath.

Now, in all the times of his many visits, I'd said nothing to the old lady, and she, in her turn had never mentioned him walking into her garden and becoming a pain in the backside! Finally, over a cup of coffee, I'd had enough and asked her if she would have a word with the old chap to stay away while I was there, before I lost my temper with him. I remember her eyes arching up and she seemed very surprised at my disclosures. I suggested it was one of her next door neighbours popping in to make sure she was okay. I thought the old lady was going to pass out when I described the man; she went ashen when I told her he hobbled about on an old bent cane made out of what looked to be a sycamore branch and smoked a troublesome pipe that kept wanting to blow out.

"You have just described Edward, my husband!" she cried out. "He's been dead 11 years."

A few weeks later, the old lady passed away too.

Chapter Seven: The Posh House Gardener

On the theme of gardening, years before, when my two kids were youngsters, we had a day's outing to a very posh Northamptonshire play park/animal sanctuary, in the grounds of a country mansion – no names mentioned. While the kids went on the adventure playground, watched over by my wife Helen, I decided on a walk around a walled-in garden. Inside was fantastic with the most exotic flowers, shrubs and blooms I had ever seen, and the fragrance was out of this world.

At one end of the extensive garden and in the vegetable section, was a long greenhouse situated against a south facing wall. I admired the giant leeks, Brussels sprouts and artichokes etc, this being autumn, with all the golden tints of the leaves on the trees. We had come to this place only weeks before it was the closed season.

As I walked along the deep gravel paths, I suddenly noticed a very old chap with a straggly white beard, pushing a large, old fashioned wooden wheelbarrow with its iron wheel, on a path opposite me. It looked like jolly hard work and he seemed to be wheezing, his face partly hidden under a large floppy hat. He was wearing a shirt (sleeves rolled up) and blue overalls. His bronzed arms were very thin and bony, and the same applied to his body. I shouted across to him that he could have done with a rubber tyre on his barrow, but he ignored me and never looked my way once. Much later, on leaving the estate, I remarked to the lady in the ticket office by the main entrance that, being such a posh place as it was, and with so many visitors, could not the owners see their way clear to buying the old gardener a decent builder's wheelbarrow? I suggested it must be a killer trying to push a heavy, iron-wheeled barrow through deep gravel.

The lady looked bemused at me and told me they did not have a permanent gardener. A team of landscapers came in at regular intervals to manage the estate. When asked to describe the old chap, the colour drained from her face. Somewhere in the archives, there was a picture of an old gardener taken in the late 1800s showing him with his giant wheelbarrow!

Chapter Eight: The Witham Ghost

Quite a few years ago, when I owned a big 750 Honda motorcycle, I belonged to an archaeological group based in the village of Washingborough – a large community just south east of Lincoln, squeezed between flat fenland on one side and rolling hills on the other.

Our group was quite large and we often went field walking on nearby arable fenland – with the farmers permission of course. One day, we were at a location called '5 mile house' – a popular fishing spot with Sheffield anglers on the River Witham, which was quite wide here. We were searching fields to the left of the footbridge, and towards a pumping station building in the distance and facing Lincoln. We had no metal detectors, just eye searching. On the river bank were various people walking by at times; anglers and dog walkers.

After a long spell our team leader collected all our finds, which were mostly pottery, then declared the proceedings over. It had been a pleasant Sunday morning walk in early April, warm, bright and sunny for the time of year. On my way back to my motorbike, I noticed a pretty looking young lady with flowing ginger hair and wearing a long white dress, sat on the river bank, watching us as we walked by.

I said nothing to my companions because it was obvious they

must have seen her, she was sat only yards from the footpath. I started my bike up and make to leave the car park when I suddenly noticed the girl was walking towards me. I let my bike tick over as she strode by, a huge smile on her rather pale face. I reciprocated and then made to move off. I would say the girl was in her early twenties. The dress she had on, though, was more like an evening gown. I glanced once in my rear view mirror as I gently moved off, but couldn't see her. I immediately stopped and looked round, she had vanished without trace! Only cars and a fishermen's bus stood in the wide car park. I looked all around but there was nowhere she could have run to and hide in the brief 3 or 4 seconds I last saw her. I have never managed to establish who this girl was.

Chapter Nine: The Hackthorn Ghosts

The 'posh' village of Hackthorn lies just off the A15, about 7 miles due north of Lincoln. Back in the 1980s I weekly gardened for a wealthy family there in a sprawling property – no names mentioned.

At one stage during my time there, they went off on holiday and told me a local girl would maybe call round and feed their rabbit. They had a huge garden and the hutch and run was some way from the house amongst the flower beds.

I was working away weeding one afternoon in glorious sunny weather when I looked up to see a smartly dressed girl walking a large Red Setter dog. She had spotted me straight away. As she got closer, I noticed she was dressed oddly. She had a white frill blouse on, satin black waistcoat, long black skirt and knee high boots. Her dark hair was held by a net at the back. She looked as though she had come from a horse dressage event, where the women sit side-saddle. In her hand was a long black cane with a shiny silver cap. Just looking at her told me she was a toff and daughter of some rich aristocrat. She refused to speak when I said a polite "hello".

I watched her walk all round the garden, stopping now and then to look at something that caught her eye, her well-groomed dog walking dutifully behind her. Eventually, she stopped by the rabbit hutch, and suddenly, to my horror, she began to violently jab her stick at the mesh.

"Hoi!" I bellowed and got up and marched toward her. She looked disdainfully at me before storming off towards the house. All the doors and gates were locked, so she wouldn't get in. I quickly checked the poor rabbit was okay, then at the fleeing pair, but I got a huge shock when I realised I was alone in the garden! She'd had no time to reach the house as it was still a long way in front of her. Although I searched all over that day, I never found them.

I reported my findings to the owners when they returned, and the lady went quite pale when I described the girl, but would not comment, only to say it was not the friends' daughter they had been relying on. Shortly after this incident I left because the family became very hostile towards me.

Chapter Ten: Buckley Green - Haworth

I began with Brontë country and will end there! My very last experience came towards the end of the research into the Susannah Shackleton puzzle. In fact it was true to say this was a most infuriating, senseless, annoying encounter through confronting a mystery person I'm still not sure was real or unreal.

My story beings in 2009. As a drystone waller, I pride myself on doing a good job every time to showcase my skills with stone. I spend many hours up in the Haworth area, studying different walling techniques. Some of the walls look fantastic, straight as a dye, with even copestones throughout the length of a given wall. However, some others look like they have been built by a gang of drunks, and look both unsightly and dangerous. A third category is, of course, an ancient wall built long, long ago, and just starting to crumble and fall, either as a result of animal intervention, such as the black faced sheep, who love jumping walls, or inclement weather such as severe frost or heavy rain, and lastly, human involvement, ie 'hoodies' who find fun throwing stones off walls. One such wall in perhaps the ancient category suffering animal intervention was in the Buckley Green area of Stanbury, near Haworth.

It is well off the beaten track of most tourists and lies beside a rutted and stony lane that falls off a hillside to join a junction with the road to Ponden Kirk – with the large reservoir just beyond. (Ponden Hall close by.)

Coming down this track one day, I noticed about a dozen stones of all shapes and sizes were laid in a bed of stinging nettles, fallen from an otherwise perfect and neat wall. Just above was a barbed wire fence and I noticed a horse grazing nearby. It may or may not have been responsible for the damage. Looking around me to make sure no-one was watching me, I gallantly picked up the stones – some very heavy, and placed them back in the wall, which looked to be around 5 feet high. I smiled to myself when I'd finished after about ten minutes, and got the tight coping stones locked into place. I assured myself that bit of wall would not move in a hurry!

About six months later, found me walking along the same track, but this time in an upwards direction from Ponden Reservoir. Imagine my shock and disgust when I came to 'my' section of wall, and saw every stone I'd carefully placed, back on the floor! What really shocked me was the fact they were all indeed in the same position as the first time!

After much head scratching, I again lifted all the stones back in place, but this time made sure there was a good 'batter'. This is stone terminology for a good angle of lean inwards to prevent collapse.

It was another year before I came to Buckley Green again, this time taking a short cut from 'Top Withins' (Wuthering Heights) to Ponden Mill for coffee and cake. Coming downhill I suddenly swore like a trooper as again I saw the wall was down! And, once again, the fallen stones were lying in exactly the same position in the nettles! I glared all around, I was sure someone was winding me up from one of the nearby farms, knocking my stones off as soon as my back was turned. But how did they manage to get them in the same position?

Once again, for a third time, I rebuilt the wall, making the angle of lean even steeper. I scowled at two horses watching me intently, I was certain they were to blame! Then and there, towards the end of my long weekend in Haworth, I vowed to return. If my wall was down again, I would soon be angrily knocking on a few doors, I hated being made a fool of.

Unbelievably, my luck was in, I caught a person full in the act – or rather after the deed! Coming down the steep track I spotted a strangely dressed woman bending over the fallen stones and appearing to be looking for something on the good part of the wall. She seemed to be wearing a kind of shawl over her head and what I took to be a shabby long coat, but as I got closer I saw it was a long skirt, almost down to her ankles.

I remember shouting, "Hey you ..... what the hell do you think you are playing at?"

The woman looked up and quickly took to her heels, me in hot pursuit. She was some way ahead but I had the advantage of running down the hill. I had almost caught her up as she reached the road junction, looked back at me, then darted left, heading to Ponden Hall in the distance. Seconds later, I reached the same spot but was shocked to the core to see the road, and a steep grassy bank devoid of human life! I ran over to the reservoir but there was nowhere to hide over the wall as the water level was lapping just below the rim. Where on earth had she gone? Muttering to myself, I retraced my steps and angrily surveyed my precious stones in the nettles again – in the same position!

I knew then this was no fluke – no person, however brainy, could place the heavy stones in the same position time after time. I decided to check the stones I'd never disturbed. To my amazement, when I ruffled through the 'hearting' (the filler in the centre of the wall), my fingers closed over a rusting, metal object. To my surprise, I saw it was an old ring, but badly corroded by time and the elements. I wondered if this was what the woman had been desperately searching for?

After a while of pondering, and a deep sigh, I once again rebuilt the wall, this time just plonking them on, my enthusiasm long gone. I placed the ring on a coping stone and then left.

During 2011, I again visited the site at Buckley Green but in the company of a local woman. To my delight I saw the wall intact, but of the rusty old ring, there was no sign. I said nothing to my companion as we walked on by. Was the tormented woman a ghost looking for her lover's lost ring, or a local woman out to cause mischief to a wall built by someone she'd fallen out with in the past? Sadly, I will never know, I avoid the place now like the plague!

OTHER PEOPLE'S STORIES (2)
RAF Digby and North Carlton

North Carlton

A lady garden customer I work for on a weekly basis, has told me of the presence of a 'white lady' on the stairs and landing of her large home on the outskirts of this little village 2½ miles east of Saxilby, where I live. They became aware of her presence some time ago when their grown up daughter Lucy, heard her name being called out in the middle of the night. Thinking it was her mum calling her, she sleepily got up and went towards her parents room. She came face to face with a woman dressed in white stood on the landing. In the instant she realised it was not her mum, the figure slowly faded away.

Since that time, the family have had numerous visitations over the years, sometimes all their Christian names being called out, including Lucy's dad. However, there is always a feeling of deep peace when this apparition is about. And maybe I have sampled her too! Very recently, in mid-April this year, I was re-edging and weeding their front gravel driveway. I was on my hands and knees (using a kneeling mat) pulling out long grass, weeds and dandelions from the edges.

Suddenly, just for a few seconds, a beautiful aroma of some

exotic perfume blew over me,   no-one was in evidence and no shrub or nearby bush could have produced such a delectable, overpowering smell, and the air was dead calm. All too soon, the aroma vanished. I told the lady of the house and suggested, just maybe, it could belong to her 'white lady'!

RAF Digby

During the warmer months of 2011, I was sat having a meal in the 'Garden Carvery' off the A15 Lincoln to Sleaford road. It is about 5 miles due south of Lincoln and situated on the hard-standing of a former RAF fighter airfield of World War II, RAF Coleby Grange.

The nearby control tower, still almost intact, is said to be heavily haunted by a high-ranking officer who stands by the railings on the top floor and looking out over the deserted airfield.

While eating my meal, I got into conversation with an elderly couple at the next table, and told them about the legend of the control tower and my own experiences on haunted airfields. To my surprise, the couple told me of their own, one-and-only confrontation with ghosts.

Many years previously, one sunny, Sunday afternoon, they were out for a leisurely drive down a narrow country lane not far from the former Spitfire airfield of RAF Digby. No traffic was on the road as they drove at a sedate pace. Suddenly though, the old chap had to literally stand on his brakes to avoid what he said, were 12 young men in flying gear and Mae West life jackets, running across the road in front of them before vanishing into an impenetrable Hawthorn hedge!

I have since studied an ordnance survey map and indeed there is a by-way of sorts running close by what was the top end of the airfield, now used as a wireless and radar establishment, and run by the RAF. In wartime, there could have been young pilots running to their parked spitfires, on a 'scramble', ready to do battle with the German Luftwaffe.

The couple were adamant at what they saw, and I have no reason to disbelieve them.

* There is just one other story, way back in the '60s, about a haunted Lincolnshire church that I'm not allowed to publish in this book, because it already appears in a ghost book by a lady author in Bath, called 'True Ghost Stories of our time' by Vivienne Rae-Ellis. It concerns blood dripping down stone steps in the tower!

CONCLUSION

During my lifetime thus far of 67 years, I have had so many encounters with spirits on and off the haunted airfields. In all respects I was relaxed and carefree prior to all the visitations by folk from another time. I was simply Joe Public going about their everyday business with not a hint of what was to befall me.

My 'best' encounters of course, happened in Brontë country, but the Susannah Shackleton mystery still remains unsolved after 14 years, despite folk helping me from many quarters. By far the most baffling though, was the Buckley Green incident, when the fallen stones from the drystone wall landed exactly in the same position as the first time I came across them! And who was the mystery woman in the dowdy clothes, searching the top of the wall?

The rusty ring had gone on my very last visit and the wall still intact, and she got what she wanted, but how did it become buried deep in the wall? Had she spurned her former lover and threw it over the wall, but it accidentally fallen between the copestones? And in Lincolnshire, who was the phantom horseman who could barely walk, and the lack of noise from the old cart? I'll never know.

The only encounter I find I have difficulty with, is the old chap who regularly came into that garden to chat with me. <u>NO</u> spirit is capable of speech, and I tend to think the old lady was a bit confused when she claimed it was her dead husband, even though the clothes and description I gave her of him, tallied. I'll have to go 50-50 on this issue because I'm not sure either way. What do you think – ghost or real?!

I think, out of all my experiences, the one that remains vividly with me to this day, is the 'angry' young lady of Haworth! If she spotted that pound coin, why didn't she take it before I had chance to. And of course, why did she look so grumpy at me, the stranger? On the night of the Torchlight Procession, I'd simply smiled at her. Had she had a bust-up with a boyfriend, husband? Did she view me as a pervert?! Or was she just too 'posh' to speak to me, a lower class working man?

I peep into the 'Apothecary' every Christmas I go up to Haworth, but I have never seen that girl from that day in Church Lane, to this.